ULYSSES S. GRANT

and the Road to Appomattox

Richard Sapp

WORLD ALMANAC® LIBRARY

Please visit our web site at: www.worldalmanaclibrary.com
For a free color catalog describing World Almanac® Library's list of high-quality books
and multimedia programs, call 1-800-848-2928 (USA) or 1-800-387-3178 (Canada).
World Almanac® Library's fax: (414) 332-3567.

Library of Congress Cataloging-in-Publication Data

Sapp, Richard.
    Ulysses S. Grant and the road to Appomattox / Richard Sapp.
       p. cm. — (In the footsteps of American heroes)
    Includes bibliographical references and index.
    ISBN 0-8368-6431-X (lib. bdg.)
    ISBN 0-8368-6436-0 (softcover)
    1. Grant, Ulysses S., 1822-1885—Military leadership—Juvenile literature.
2. Generals—United States—Biography—Juvenile literature. 3. United States.
Army—Biography—Juvenile literature. 4. Appomattox Campaign, 1865—
Juvenile literature. I. Title. II. Series.
    E672.S27   2006
    937.7'41092—dc22
  [B]   2005054471

First published in 2006 by
World Almanac® Library
A Member of the WRC Media Family of Companies
330 West Olive Street, Suite 100
Milwaukee, WI 53212 USA

Copyright © 2006 by World Almanac® Library.

Produced by Compendium Publishing Ltd
First Floor, 43 Frith Street
London W1D 4SA

For Compendium Publishing
Editor: Don Gulbrandsen
Picture research: Mindy Day and Sandra Forty
Design: Ian Hughes/Compendium Design
Artwork: Mark Franklin

World Almanac® Library managing editor: Valerie J. Weber
World Almanac® Library editor: Leifa Butrick
World Almanac® Library art direction: Tammy West
World Almanac® Library production: Jessica Morris and Robert Kraus

Photo Credits: Corbis: pages 1, 7(T), 8, 18(T), 19 (C&B), 23(T), 33, 37(T), 42, 48(T), and 55(B);
Library of Congress: cover, chapter openers, and pages 7(B), 9, 12–17 (all), 18(B), 19(T), 20, 26, 28,
29, 31, 32, 37(B), 44, 46, 48(B), 51–54 (all), 57; Getty Images: 10, 22, 23(B), 25, 30, 34, 35, 36, 38
(both), 40, 41, 43, 46, 49, 55(T), 56(both), 60, 61

Printed in the United States of America

1 2 3 4 5 6 7 8 9 10 09 08 07 06

CONTENTS

COVER AND CHAPTER OPENINGS: This photograph of Ulysses S. Grant was taken at Cold Harbor, Virginia in August 1864. Grant was forty-two years old and the commander of the Union army. He was facing the last eight months of the Civil War.

TITLE PAGE: This hand-colored engraving by Alonzo Chappel depicts General Ulysses S. Grant commander of the Union army during the Civil War. Grant is sitting on a box of ammunition, studying a map, and planning his next campaign against the Confederate army.

INTRODUCTION

I n this book, we follow Ulysses S. Grant's journey from a listless young boy to the successful commander of the Union forces during the Civil War. The map (*righ* shows significant places on this journey. Throughout the text, sidebars describe these locations. The book traces the footsteps of Ulysses Grant and highlights important Civil War locations, many of them marked today by museums, parks, or protected sites.

Ulysses S. Grant

The history of the United States is filled with stories of seemingly ordinary people who, when faced with incredib challenges, accomplished extraordinary things. Many stories tell of people who failed time and time again but kept after their goal and eventually achieved success beyond their wildest imagination. These are the stories that support the concept of the American Dream—the belief that anything is possible with hard work, focus, and persistence.

Ulysses S. Grant's life is a classic tale of the American Dream. Many people remember that Grant was a Civil War general and later president of the United States, but that is only part of the story. Ulysses S. Grant was not always famous or heroic or important. For much of his life, he seemed like an ordinary, unimportant person, especially in his own eyes. At certain times, he seemed to be a complete failure. As a boy, he was not a particular good student. After becoming an army officer, he often found himself assigned to difficult or unpopular duties, and, at one point, he was forced to resign in disgrace. He tried to farm and go into business for himself, but he had trouble supporting his family.

Then, in the 1860s, the United States faced one of its greatest crises—the Civil War. This conflict split the nation into two parts—the North, or Union, versus the South, or Confederacy. Suddenly, the United States needed Ulysses S. Grant, and he seemed to discover his purpose in life. Although the course of his early life had been uncertain, he started on an amazing journey during the Civil War that changed United States' history. When the Union appeared to be losing the war and the chances for a reunited nation were slight, Grant gave the country hope. Commanding forces in the West, Grant calmly and patiently led his troops to victory after victory. When the nation needed a leader to bring the war to a timely end, it called Grant to the East. He responded by directing a brilliant campaign to defeat the Confederacy. When Americans needed a president to help them heal after the war, they called on Grant, and he served two terms in the White House.

Long before he began his journey to the White House, Ulysses Grant was a simple, quiet boy from Ohio who loved horses, and the United States was struggling to overcome differences between its citizens that threatened to tear it apart. That is where this journey begins.

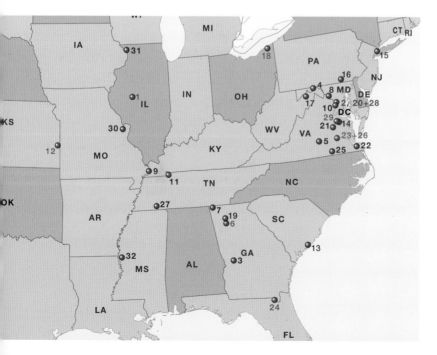

On this map, the green dots represent the places mentioned in the sidebars. The red dots represent important Civil War sites described in Places to Visit or Research on pages 58 and 59. The addresses, Web sites, and telephone numbers of all the numbered sites are listed in Places to Visit or Research.

CHAPTER 1
GRANT'S EARLY YEARS

Hiram Ulysses Grant (the name of the future presiden at birth) was born on April 27, 1822, in a two-room cabin on the Ohio River in Point Pleasant, Ohio. Grant's family had been in the United States for eight generations. His father, Jesse, had little education, but he was an avid reader and made a good living from the tannery he owned. Jesse was a tall, brash man, a talkative Yankee who stood out in the quiet, slow-paced town just north of the Mason-Dixon line.

Ulysses was very different from his father. He was small, thin, and quiet—even shy—by nature. Some people thought he was dull and, rather than use his nickname, "Lis," referred to him as "Listless." Unlike many boys of his era, Ulysses did not enjoy sports, and he never hunted He was known for his proper behavior and for his refusal to use coarse language. "Doggone it" was the closest Ulysses ever came to swearing. In school, Ulysses was a poor student; math was his best subject by far. Ulysses ha no desire to go into the tanning business; he was sickened by the sight and smell of the tannery's bloody hides.

He may have had shortcomings, but Ulysses also had a special passion—he was a gifted horseman. He could ride any animal, bareback or saddled, and he could get it to run faster or work harder than anybody else could. Families in his neighborhood hired him to tame their horses. After Jesse Grant bought land outside of town with profits from the tannery business, Ulysses spent most of his time working alone on the farm, quietly plowing and hauling wood with his horses.

Jesse sent Ulysses away to boarding school for two winters, but the experience did not improve Ulysses' stud abits. His chief desire was to escape the annery; he hoped to become a farmer, trader, or a mathematics teacher instead. Realizing that he would never convince his son to stay in the family business, Jesse decided to pursue glory for him in other ways. Without Ulysses' knowledge, Jesse secured an appointment to the U.S. Military Academy for his son. Initially, Ulysses refused to go, but his father insisted. In 1839, at the age of seventeen, he boarded a steamship and left his home for West Point, New York.

West Point

Some confusion arose about Ulysses' name when he was in the process of entering the military academy. His initials—H.U.G.— embarrassed him and prompted teasing from other children during his youth. He saw an opportunity to start fresh at West Point, so he changed his name to Ulysses S. Grant. Many people have wrongly assumed that the "S" in his name stood for "Simpson," his mother's maiden name, but Grant admitted that the initial stood for nothing. Of course, the initials "U.S." led to new nicknames for the future president. Cadets at the U.S. Military Academy wondered if "U.S." stood for "United States" or "Uncle Sam," and soon they started calling him "Sam."

"Sam" was never very enthusiastic about the military academy. The military life and its constant drilling and unusual attention to clean uniforms and grooming did not suit him well. He was an average student and graduated from West Point in 1843, ranking twenty-first out of thirty-nine cadets in his class. Not surprisingly, he was the best

Grant's parents, Hanna Simpson and Jesse Root Grant

horseman and, throughout his time at West Point, was happiest when he could put on dirty, old clothes and spend time on horseback.

Upon graduation, Lieutenant Ulysses Grant was assigned to the Fourth Infantry in St. Louis, Missouri, which happened to be the hometown of his West Point roommate, Frederick Dent. Grant's duties were not challenging, and he often rode 12 miles (19 kilometers) to socialize at the Dent family farm, called White Haven. There, he me his future bride, Frederick's sister Julia. Before he left for his next assignment, they were engaged.

War With Mexico

In 1844, the Fourth Infantry was transferred to Louisiana. Six months later, Grant's regimen was sent to Corpus Christi, Texas as part of a three thousand-man

Sketch of Grant as a second lieutenant shortly after his graduation from West Point in 1843

force led by future president Zachary Taylor. The purpose of the massed U.S. troops was clear: to provoke a war with Mexico that might allow the United States to annex Mexican territory. Privately, Grant was unhappy with the political situation. He thought the impending war would be an unfair act of a large, strong nation taking advantag of a smaller, weaker country. Nonetheless, he behaved like the perfect soldier, marching south into Mexico and towar inevitable conflict.

During the invasion, Grant served as regimental quartermaster. He was responsible for making sure that soldiers had food, clothing, and equipment. This was important work, but it was difficult and anything but glamorous. Frustrated, Grant applied for a transfer but

Grant's signature

as denied. He
emed destined
 spend the war
anaging
agonloads of
pplies far from
e front lines.
  Grant may not
ave agreed with
e aims of the
ar, but he was
ger to see action.
s the invasion
rce, which now
umbered nearly
x thousand men,
pproached
onterrey, Mexico,
rant ignored
ders and moved
 the front to
atch artillery
und the city.
uddenly, Zachary
aylor ordered
oops to charge,
d Grant found
mself swept up
 the attack. Two
ays later, Grant

Grant at the Capture of the City of Mexico. **Grant fought well in the Mexican War but found peacetime soldiering difficult.**

as among the soldiers trapped in the city by Mexican
rces and running low on ammunition. He bravely
sponded to a request for a volunteer to travel by horse
 the main U.S. forces. His amazing riding skills paid
f, and he was able to elude Mexican sharpshooters
d get help. The U.S. forces soon captured Monterrey.
  Despite his heroism, Grant was quickly returned to
s quartermaster duties when the invasion moved south
ward Mexico City. While several of his West Point
assmates—including Frederick Dent—earned promotions

for their actions, Grant remained a second lieutenant, seemingly unnoticed by his superiors. Then, in the final assault on Mexico City, Grant distinguished himself again. He had the idea of mounting a large gun in a church tower; from its high position, he was able to decimate the Mexican troops hiding below and turn the tide of the battle. General William Worth noted Grant's sharp thinking, and soon Ulysses was rewarded with a promotion.

Disgrace

Mexico and the war left a lasting mark on Grant, and he fondly talked about his experiences for many years.

After the war, Grant, now captain, returned to St. Louis and married Julia Dent. She accompanied him to posts in New York and Michigan. The young military couple was happy. When Julia became pregnant, she returned to her parents' home in St. Louis to give birth to their son, Frederick Dent Grant. Ulysses was sent back to New York, and the growing Grant family settled happily there; Julia was soon expecting another baby.

In the spring of 1852, Grant's situation changed dramatically. Grant and his regiment received orders to transfer to Oregon. The West Coast was booming, thanks to the recent California gold rush. Grant knew it would

Grant with his wife Julia, shown in a photograph taken around 1860

be impossible to take his family with him and considered resigning from the army. He realized, however, that giving up his career would be unwise at that point in his life, so he took the long journey to the West Coast—by ship to Panama, overland through the jungle, and then on to another ship to their new post at Fort Vancouver, Oregon.

Grant's time in Oregon was difficult. The army had little to do, and he did not have much contact with his beloved

mily, which now included a second child, Ulysses Jr.
rant dreamed of moving his family west to live with
im, but he did not earn enough to support them in a
art of the country where the gold rush had inflated
rices far beyond normal. He tried investing in a couple
moneymaking schemes, but they failed. He thought
gain of quitting the army.

In 1853, Grant was transferred to Fort Humboldt in
orthern California. This outpost was even smaller and
nelier than Fort Vancouver, and Grant did not get along
ith the commanding officer. Soon he turned to whiskey to
eal with his unhappiness. When an investment in a pool
all failed, he started drinking more and even showed up
runk for duty. In April 1854, Grant's commanding officer
rced him to resign his commission, threatening to put
im on trial for drunkenness. He left the army in disgrace
ter a fifteen-year career and returned to St. Louis with
money, no job, and few prospects for the future.

Julia's father, a blustering slave owner who liked to be
lled Colonel Dent, had given her 60 acres (24 hectares)
ear St. Louis as a wedding present. Grant took his family
ere, built a cabin, and began to farm and cut wood. He
orked hard, but it soon became apparent that Sam Grant
as no farmer. The family was forced to move to White
aven to live with Julia's family. Grant's health worsened
he suffered from ague, a disease similar to malaria, that

Grant's log cabin, "Hardscrabble," on the White Haven grounds. He built it by hand, and he and his family lived there for three months until his mother-in-law's death when they moved into White Haven.

FORT SUMTER NATIONAL MONUMENT

The Civil War began on April 12, 1861, at this site, located on an island in the Charleston, South Carolina, harbor (map reference 13). There is a new visitor center on the mainland from which visitors can access the fort; a park ferry and private tour boats both provide service to the island. The preserved fort features a museum, and nearby Fort Moultrie is also part of the monument. In addition, efforts are under way to preserve nearby Morris Island, site of the famous battle fought by the African American 54th Massachusetts Infantry and featured in the movie *Glory*.

he caught in Panama. He sold off belongings to support his family, he took out loans, and he worked a succession of short-term jobs. He even ran for public office . . . and lost. The Grant family fell into poverty.

By 1860, the Grants were penniless, and Ulysses needed to help his family. Desperate, he borrowed money for a railroad ticket to Ohio, where he asked his father for a job in the hated family tanning business. Jesse Grant saw his thirty-seven-year-old son as a failure, but he would not turn his back on Ulysses. Jesse arranged for the future president to work for his younger brothers, Simpson and Orvil, as a lowly clerk in the family leather-goods business in Galena, Illinois.

Grant was not a particularly good clerk (he had trouble remembering the price of things), but life was more secure and he could spend ample time with the family he loved so much. For a year, the Grants lived quietly in Galena.

In 1860, Abraham Lincoln was elected president, and the state of South Carolina seceded (withdrew) from the Union. Ten other Southern states also eventually seceded from the United States and formed the independent Confederate States of America with their capital at Richmond, Virginia. On April 12, 1861, General Beauregard, in command of the provisional Confederate forces, attacked U.S. troops that Lincoln had sent to occupy Fort Sumter. War had begun.

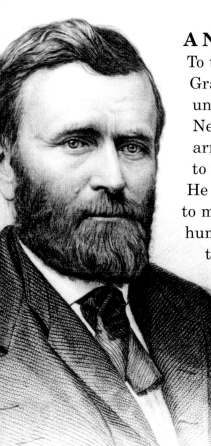

A New Command

To the quiet but sensible Grant, the war was unwelcome news. Nevertheless, as a former army officer, he felt obligated to volunteer his services. He also saw the opportunity to make amends for his humiliating resignation from the army. Two companies of Galena men signed up to fight, but only one man in town had ever served in the regular military— U.S. Grant. Soon he was drilling the Illinois volunteers to get them ready for service.

Grant marched the volunteers to the capitol in Springfield and tried to secure an appointment as an army officer; none came. The competition was fierce in the politically charged climate, and Grant's damaged reputation came back to haunt him. He became frustrated and traveled to Ohio in search of an officer's rank. The results were no better. Then, while Grant was in Ohio, he was appointed— without being consulted—colonel in charge of the Twenty-first Illinois, a ragtag outfit desperately in need of leadership. The troops made fun of their new colonel's rumpled appearance and openly mocked him. Grant patiently accepted the jabs and soon gave them a taste of regular army training. Before long, he had earned their loyalty and drilled them into a legitimate military unit— and none too soon. Battle with Confederate forces loomed in the near future.

This engraving by John C. Buttre shows Grant as a general. He became brigadier general in 1861 and was promoted major general of volunteers in 1862. He was promoted to lieutenant general after defeating the Confederates at Lookout Mountain on November 25, 1863. Soon after, President Abraham Lincoln named him general in chief of all Union armies.

CHAPTER 2
A GROWING RIFT

During the nineteenth century, many people moved to the United States hoping for a new and better life. Refugees from war and famine in Europe and Asia flooded into the North, looking for work and riches. Other people, kidnapped in Africa and sold, were forcibly dragged in chains to the South. There, they were resold at public auctions as slaves. Most were purchased by plantation owners and were forced to work very hard in cotton and tobacco fields. They were fed poorly, beaten savagely for small infractions of the rules, and paid nothing for their labor. Slaves had no rights as citizens or human beings.

The country was growing rapidly westward, and the question arose whether to allow slavery in the new territories. Many people in the industrial North thought slavery should be abolished. Southern plantation owners, however, thought slaves were an economic necessity. In 1820, the Missouri Compromise brought Missouri and Maine into the union—Missouri as a slave state and Maine as a free state. This move balanced the number of states voting as a block—slave states versus free—in the U.S. Senate, where each state had two votes.

A new way of thinking about the nation had also slowly taken hold of the popular imagination after 1803. That year, President Thomas Jefferson purchased the vast Louisiana Territories and sent Meriwether Lewis and William Clark exploring to the West Coast. The Louisiana Purchase opened millions of acres of land to settlement. In the 1840s, the United States invaded Mexico and annexed Texas and the Southwest, including California, to fulfill what people had come to believe was its "manifest destiny."

New states began to form as settlers flooded over the

palachian Mountains in the East and down the Ohio
ver. These people envisioned free lives, independent
ms, and their own businesses. Migrants from the South
rried with them the belief that slaves were inferior
man beings and that slavery was both acceptable
d enshrined in the U.S. Constitution.

Decade Of Crisis

ring the 1850s, the United States lurched from crisis to
sis. In the North, abolitionists aroused the public's moral
dignation about slavery. Other reformers wanted free
blic schools built for all children and increased government
ersight of utilities, factories, canals, and railroads.
In the South, equally vocal crusaders preached that the
ht to own slaves was guaranteed by law. They declared
it the federal government should concern itself only with
tional defense and that each state should be allowed to
velop its own way of life according to its individual
nscience and political will.

Many businesses in the South had come to depend on free labor provided by slaves.

The Underground Railroad. **This 1893 painting by Charles T. Webber illustrates the hardships that runaway slaves endured on their route to freedom. Poorly clothed, they traveled by foot through snow, cold, and dangerous territories.**

Six developments hastened the start of the war that consumed the United States from 1861 until 1865:

• In 1850, the U.S. Congress passed the Fugitive Slave Act. This law gave owners the right to seize runaway slaves anywhere they were found. The act obligated the police and the courts to return slaves to captivity. It imposed fines and even jail sentences upon those who aided runaways. Intended to appease Southern politician the act inflamed abolitionist passions.

• The Underground Railroad, a secret network of antislaver activists, had smuggled escaped slaves to freedom since the Revolutionary War. Black and white individuals participated including people like Harriet Tubman, an escaped slave, and members of the Society of Friends, called Quakers.

• In 1852, Harriet Beecher Stowe published *Uncle Tom's Cabin,* which portrayed the brutal life of Southern slaves. The book was an international bestseller. When Stowe lat met Abraham Lincoln, he remarked, "So you are the little lady who made this big war."

• The Kansas-Nebraska Act of 1854 gave voters in these two territories the right to choose whether they would liv in a slave state or a free state. Abolitionists and Souther: farmers flooded in, looking for new land in both territori(and often clashed violently.

ricans sold into slavery were often stripped and put on display, like animals, on the auction block.

ap of the United States showing the seceded Confederate States of America

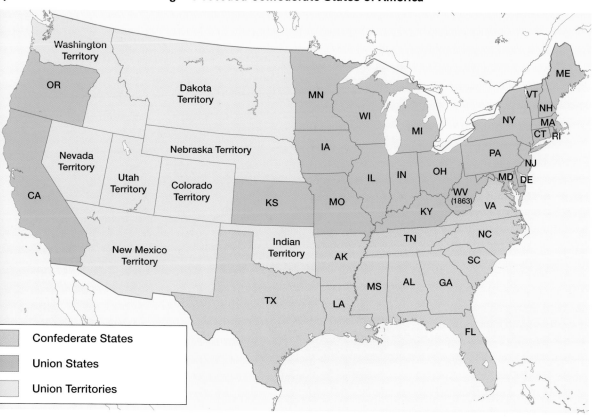

Abolitionist John Brown
around 1850 when he
would have been fifty

• In the Dred Scott case, the Supreme Court ruled in 1857 that neither slaves nor free blacks had rights as citizens. Congress, the Supreme Court declared, had no authority to limit the spread of slavery.

• In 1859, John Brown, a fiery abolitionist with blood on his hands from the fighting in Kansas, led a small group of men to attack the federal arsenal at Harpers Ferry, Virginia. He intended to seize weapons stored at the arsenal, distribute them to slaves, and start a rebellion in the process. U.S. Marines led by Colonel Robert E. Lee crushed Brown's raid. Brown was tried and hung, becoming a martyr to antislavery activists.

As Americans argued about these issues and events, positions became inflexible. As people saw their livelihoods and self-images threatened, emotions were easily involved. When the nation elected Abraham Lincoln as president— a man who had spoken out against slavery—armed conflict became unavoidable.

One of the major differences between the North and South was their level of industrialization. Factories sprang up in the North, creating wealth, urbanization, and employment. The South was a more land-based society and had become used to unpaid slave labor. This 1854 print shows the Manchester Print Works, a thriving Northern industry in Manchester, New Hampshire.

HARPERS FERRY NATIONAL HISTORICAL PARK

This park, located at the scenic confluence of the Shenandoah and Potomac rivers (map reference 17), is rich with history but is best known for its connection to abolitionist John Brown. Visiting tourists can see the area's museums, take part in ranger-guided tours, or enjoy one of the park's many special events to learn more about this important site and its role in shaping the United States. Activities every October mark the anniversary of John Brown's failed raid on the federal arsenal.

The Harpers Ferry insurrection is depicted by this sequence of illustrations. The first (*above*) shows government forces–U.S. Marines under the command of Robert E. Lee–retaking the arsenal on October 18, 1859, two days after John Brown and his followers took it. The second (*center*) shows the prison and courthouse in Charleston, Virginia, where John Brown and the other Harpers Ferry prisoners were held and tried. The third (*below*) shows John Brown ascending the scaffold during his execution on December 2, 1859. Although John Brown was tried and hanged, his actions generated sympathy for the abolitionist cause.

CHAPTER 3
THE WAR BEGINS

U lysses Grant's Civil War service began in the heartland, where the Mississippi and Ohio Rivers join together near the borders of Illinois, Kentucky, and Missouri. Thanks to an Illinois congressma who thought his state had too few generals, Grant was soon promoted to brigadier general.

Departing from Cairo, Illinois, in November 1861, Grant led his small army against Confederate forces at Belmont, Missouri. The battle was relatively unimportant and indecisive, but more than fifteen hundred men were killed or wounded. Grant maintained that this first battle gave him and his raw troops an important sense of what was ahead. He survived acute personal danger, and his soldiers acquired confidence in themselves that served them well over the next three years.

The war had begun with high expectations on both sides. Confederate and Union leaders believed that the fighting would be over by the end of 1861, and each side believed that it would be victorious. Grant, although he was stationed in the West, thought the war would be decided in the East, but the early fighting there did not go well for the Union.

President Lincoln struggled to find a competent commander

his Army of the Potomac, just as Jefferson Davis ... rched for the best man to lead his Army of Northern ...rginia. Leadership of these powerful armies would be ...cial to either side's success. Davis initially handed the ...ns of his army to P. G. T. Beauregard, while General ...nfield Scott led the Union army. Scott had enjoyed ...uccessful military career; Ulysses Grant had served ...der him during the Mexican War. Scott was seventy-...e years old, however, and not up to directing a war ...npaign. A new field leader had to be identified quickly.

The Union army had other problems. Although it was a ...fessional fighting force, it was very small. Additionally, ...ny of its best officers had been Southerners who joined ... Confederate army when their states seceded.

In May, 1861, a month after Fort Sumter was attacked, ...tt appointed Irvin McDowell to lead the Union troops. ...ving to political pressure, Scott ordered McDowell to ...e his soldiers into battle. Enthusiastic recruits rushed to ...end the Stars and Stripes and to trample the rebellion, ... they barely knew how to load and fire their weapons.

As the Union army assembled, hopes were high for a short war. Soldiers, generals, and political leaders could not know the war would last four long years.

Established in 1940, this 5,000-acre (2,023-ha) park (map reference 21), not far from Washington, D.C., commemorates the site of two major battles—both Confederate victories—fought in 1861 and 1862. These events are known as the battles of Bull Run in the annals of Northern history. Civil War battles often have two names, one from Union records and one from the Confederates'. Union names often related to a body of water, while Confederates thought of the closest town. Bull Run is the creek that runs through the park along which the battles were fought. Confederates called them the battles of Manassas after a nearby settlement.

The equestrian statue of "Stonewall" Jackson looks over Henry Hill toward the battlefields of Manassas (Bull Run).

When McDowell and Beauregard confronted one another in northern Virginia at Bull Run (the First Battle of Manassas) on July 21, 1861, thousands of sightseers rode out from Washington with picnic baskets to watch the charges and the bombardments. The horror of that day's slaughter, with more than five thousand men killed, wounded, and captured, ended the sightseeing. Although Union General McDowell came remarkably close to victory, his inexperienced men eventually turned and ran. The Confederates were stunned by this turn of events and could not capitalize on their victory. The demoralized Union army fled to Washington, in some cases arriving before the terrified picnickers.

Jefferson Davis was disappointed in Beauregard's failure to take further advantage of this victory, so he replaced him with Joe Johnston. When Johnston was severely wounded at the battle of Seven Pines in 1862, Davis chose Robert E. Lee, the most capable military commander of the era and the man who would be Grant's main opponent in the last years of the war.

Ironically, Lee was asked to lead both the Union and Confederate forces. Lee was born in 1807. His father, "Light Horse" Harry Lee, was a Virginia planter and Revolutionary War hero. Related to George Washington, the Lees were American aristocracy. Upon graduating second in his class from the U.S. Military Academy at West Point, New York, in 1829, the handsome and engaging Robert E. Lee married Mary Anne Randolph Custis, the granddaughter of George Washington.

Lee—like Grant—fought under General Winfield Scott during the Mexican War and was decorated for courage. Indeed, Scott later said, "Lee was the very best soldier that I ever saw in the field." After the bombardment of Fort Sumter, Scott offered Lee command of the Union armies—the very position that would take Grant some years to achieve.

Lee was ambivalent about slavery, but he believed strongly in state's rights. He said he could not imagine raising his sword against his Southern family, and he chose to fight for the Confederacy when Virginia seceded from the Union. Once Jefferson Davis gave him control of the Confederate military forces in 1862, he held the post until the end of the war.

Two great rivals: Grant (*above*) shortly after he became a brigadier general and (*left*) Robert E. Lee (1807–1870), seen in about 1845. Superficially, their military careers had similarities: Both went to West Point; both served in Mexico under Scott. Lee could have had a command in the Union army, but he chose otherwise. A brilliant general, he was revered by his men and treated with respect and courtesy by the Union forces after his surrender.

CHAPTER 4
HOPE IN THE WEST

In the North, Lincoln had turned to George McClellan to replace the hapless McDowell as leader of the Army of the Potomac after the failure at Bull Run. McClellan was a disciplined leader who drilled his troops relentlessly. He resented General Winfield Scott's oversight, however, and started contradicting the elderly general in staff meetings.

Criticism of Scott was widespread. People blamed him for the early defeats and also ridiculed his Anaconda Plan, which called for a naval blockade to strangle the Confederacy, preventing the rebels from selling their tobacco and cotton abroad or importing weapons. The blockade would give the new Union armies time to develop as fighting forces for what Scott—correctly—thought was going to be a long and difficult war. Under political pressure and in poor health, Scott retired, and, by the end of 1861, George McClellan had complete control of the Army of the Potomac.

McClellan proved reluctant to commit his troops to battle and hesitated to strike an effective blow against his enemy. He attacked the Confederate capital of Richmond by way of the peninsula between the James and York Rivers. The Peninsula Campaign of 1862 was carefully planned, and the Union army advanced within sight of Richmond, but McClellan's delays and poor decisions gave the Southern forces time to regroup and drive the Union back. The Peninsula Campaign was another failure for the North.

As 1862 progressed, President Lincoln feared for his dream of keeping America unified. The war in the East was going badly for the Union, and he had yet to find the right person to lead his army. Fortunately, the man who

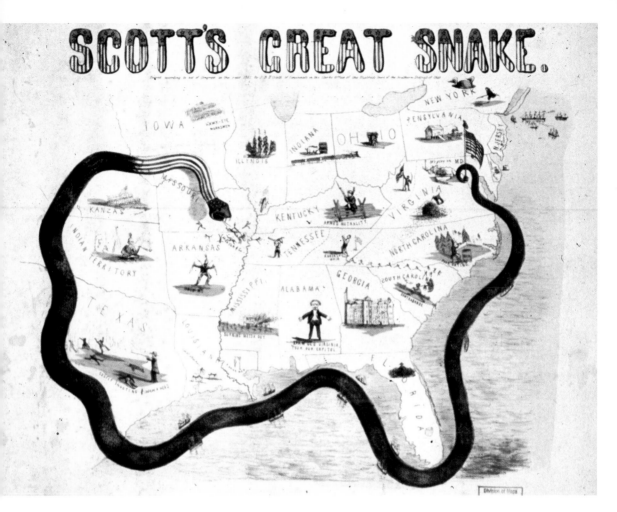

SCOTT'S GREAT SNAKE.

ould fill this role in 1864—Ulysses S. Grant—provided ray of hope with good news from the distant West.

Grant clearly understood the Anaconda Plan, created by is Mexican War commander Winfield Scott, and believed it. Grant hoped to use his troops to carry out an nportant part of the scheme. He devised a campaign to rive into the heart of the Confederacy by capturing forts long its major rivers, starting with Fort Henry on the ennessee River and Fort Donelson on the Cumberland iver. If successful, this plan would cut the South into eces and block major supply lines, just as General Scott nvisioned.

Grant had difficulty selling this plan to his superiors— nportant leaders including Major General Henry Wager alleck who still remembered Grant as a disgraced officer ith a drinking problem. Halleck finally allowed Grant— upported by 15,000 troops and, crucially, by a squadron of

Cartoon map produced in 1861 to illustrate— and ridicule—Winfield Scott's Anaconda Plan to blockade the South. Grant believed in the plan, however, and his actions in the West did much to help strangle the South.

The First Encounter of Iron-Clads. This color print of 1891 illustrates the terrific engagement between the *Monitor* and *Merrimac*.

NAVAL BLOCKADES AND IRONCLADS

As the war unfolded, President Lincoln ordered the navy to intercept all ships going to and coming from Confederate ports. Almost immediately, this blockade began to strangle the South's economy, which relied on selling cotton and tobacco in Europe. The blockade eventually halted the import of guns and ammunition for the rebellion.

In response, the South commissioned blockade runners and commerce raiders. Small and fast, blockade runners could often elude the slower, but better armed, Union vessels, and Southern commerce raiders captured scores of unarmed Northern merchant and whaling ships. Although some Confederate ships were sunk, several—the *Alabama*, *Florida*, and *Shenandoah*—were successful at moving a trickle of vital supplies to the rebels.

War on the water was highlighted by the first battles between ships plated with iron, called "ironclads." Until 1862, ships had always been made of wood, but the Confederates raised the hull of the USS *Merrimack*, a steam frigate burned when the Union navy abandoned its Norfolk Naval Yards in Virginia. The renamed CSS *Virginia* was outfitted with guns, an upper deck, a below-water-line ram, and iron plating.

On March 9, the *Virginia* attacked the Union fleet. Unwieldy and poorly designed, the rebel ironclad nevertheless destroyed two Northern warships, both wooden, before it was confronted by a Union ironclad, the USS *Monitor*. The historic battle between those iron ships ended in a draw, but that day marked the certain end of wooden navies.

The *Monitor* sank in a storm off the coast of North Carolina in 1862; its wreckage was discovered in 1973, and the site was designated a National Marine Sanctuary. The Mariner's Museum in Newport News, Virginia, (map reference 22) is developing a state-of-the-art, $30 million USS *Monitor* Center, dedicated to the era of the ironclads. It will feature artifacts recovered from the Union vessel.

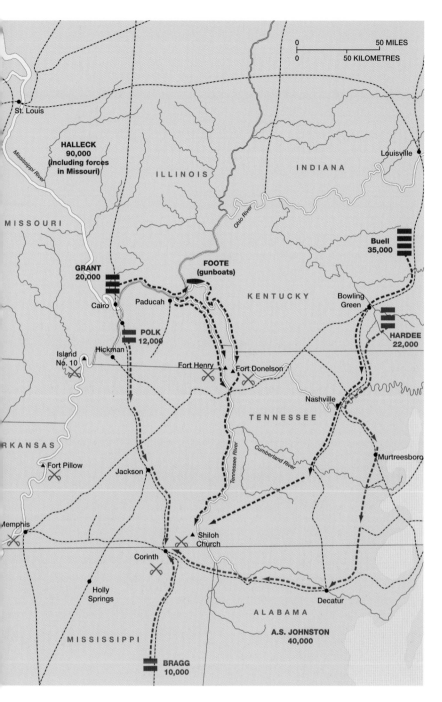

The dotted lines on the map show Grant's Union forces converging on Corinth before the battle of Shiloh. The number of soldiers each general commanded is also indicated.

FORT DONELSON NATIONAL BATTLEFIELD AND CEMETERY

This Tennessee park (map reference 11) commemorates the first major Union victory of the Civil War. Fought on a snow-covered battlefield over three cold days in February 1862, the engagement was one of the costliest of the war. There were nearly twenty thousand casualties, mostly Southern troops, and the battle opened the door for a Union invasion into the heart of the Confederacy. The battle also earned Ulysses Grant a popular, new nickname. When Union victory looked certain, the Confederate commander asked to negotiate terms of surrender. Grant replied, "No terms except an unconditional surrender can be accepted." The Southern commander and his troops surrendered, giving the Union its first hero— "Unconditional Surrender" Grant.

onclad gunboats—to put his plan into action. The unboats were commanded by Flag Officer Andrew Foote, nd their firepower proved so decisive in the first fight that he infantry was not needed. On February 6, 1862, Fort enry surrendered, and Grant immediately turned his ghts eastward to Fort Donelson.

SHILOH NATIONAL MILITARY PARK

On April 6-7, 1862, nearly 110,000 soldiers met on the banks of the Tennessee River in one of the Civil War's fiercest battles. In the end, Ulysses Grant's Union forces earned a decisive victory and then seized the nearby Confederate rail center of Corinth, Mississippi. Today the park (map reference 27) covers 4,000 acres (1,600 ha) at the battle site and includes the Shiloh National Cemetery; an interpretive center is located at Corinth.

Fort Donelson was a more difficult challenge for Grant. It was better defended than Fort Henry because Confederate General Albert Johnston had sent fifteen thousand men to boost the manpower following the fall of Fort Henry. Fort Donelson was also much better sited— Fort Henry had been on low ground that sometimes flooded; Fort Donelson was higher and better protected from the Union gunboats. Grant's land forces fought hard, and, on February 16, 1862, after a bloody three-day battle the Confederates surrendered. Grant earned a significant victory—and a new nickname: "Unconditional Surrender" Grant, thanks to his insistence that no other terms would be offered to the defenders than surrender. The hard-nosed attitude worked, and some twelve thousand Confederates walked into captivity. By all accounts, Grant remained calm and focused throughout the long and difficult battle. It appeared that Grant, the failed farmer and one-time drunk, was truly a gifted battlefield commander.

The two Union successes forced the retreat of the Confederates, who evacuated Nashville, Tennessee, and

An engraving showing the bombardment of Fort St. Philip during the battle to open the lower Mississippi and capture New Orleans.

This 1887 print shows
Grant (on horseback,
left) on February 16,
1862, during the siege of
Fort Donelson; the fort's
ramparts can be seen in
the background.

olumbus, Kentucky. Grant was promoted to major
neral. His forces swelled to forty-five thousand men,
d Halleck ordered him to push them up the Tennessee
iver toward the important railroad center of Corinth,
ississippi. There, Grant was to join another Union force
d by General Don Carlos Buell that was advancing
ward Corinth, Mississippi, from Nashville.

The Confederates saw what was happening and tried to
tack the Union armies before they could link up. Johnston
tacked Grant at Pittsburg Landing, Tennessee, along the
nks of the Tennessee River. The resulting Battle of Shiloh,
inois, on April 6–7, 1862, was the largest battle of the war
date, and both sides incurred huge losses. Ten thousand,
ven hundred Confederates and a staggering thirteen
ousand Union men were either killed or wounded. Grant
as severely criticized in the North for being caught off
ard. Grant's army was battered on April 6 and almost
feated. Rallying strongly, the Union troops held on, thanks
 the strength of Grant's defensive line and the firepower of
s gunboats. Toward night, the Union fortunes changed.
nfederate General Johnston was killed, and Buell's

Originally known as Camp Sumter, Andersonville was a Confederate prison camp notorious for maltreatment of prisoners. More than thirteen thousand prisoners died in the camp during the war. In August 1864, the camp's 26 acres (10.5 ha) held nearly thirty-three thousand prisoners.

PRISON CAMPS

Life in a Civil War prisoner-of-war camp was horrible, and the war's worst camp was located at Andersonville, Georgia. An estimated thirteen thousand men from Northern armies were starved, beaten, and left to die from exposure with no medical attention. Its commandant, Henry Wirz, pleaded that he had no supplies and little food to give the prisoners. Nevertheless, he forced them to live in the open without shelter and to drink from the stream into which their excrement ran. In 1865, Wirz was tried for war crimes and hung, the only person so tried and executed following the war.

It is estimated that fifty-six thousand men died in Union and Confederate prisons. The camp at Andersonville was shocking, but other Confederate camps such as Libby Prison in Richmond were just as bad. Union prisons such as that near Elmira, New York, were better, but barely. Today Andersonville has been preserved as a national historic site (map reference 3). A national cemetery and the recently opened National Prisoner of War Museum on the site stand as a somber tribute to men and women who served the United States in all of its wars and served time in captivity.

forces began to arrive. The next day, Grant turned the table completely and drove the Confederates back toward Corint

Shiloh was a major victory and, farther south, the U. S Navy won another important battle. On April 24, Admiral David Farragut stormed into New Orleans and advanced up the Mississippi from the south. By now, Halleck had more than one hundred thousand men under his comman and the Confederates left Corinth without a fight. Everything, it seemed, was ready for a Union advance.

Union Command Problems

Back in the East, President Lincoln struggled to find the right man to lead the Union forces, in general, and the Army of the Potomac, in particular. George McClellan was stripped of his position of general in chief after the botched Peninsular Campaign and the political backbiting that accompanied it. In July, Lincoln called Halleck to Washington and made him general in chief. Lincoln had seen the success of the armies of the West and thought Halleck was responsible for the victories.

The South, on the other hand, while hampered by a lack of supplies and other problems, never seemed to lack great military leaders. One of these leaders was Thomas J. "Stonewall" Jackson, whose Army of the Shenandoah had defeated several Union armies and earned him a formidable reputation. When a Union army led by John Pope advanced toward a second battle at Bull Run in August 1862, Jackson's smaller force held its ground until James Longstreet's twenty-eight thousand troops could arrive and launch a surprise counterattack. The North lost the second battle at Bull Run with heavy casualties. Yankee soldiers were brave and willing, but their generals let them down.

Lincoln faced massive difficulties and not only with weak army commanders. Popular enthusiasm for a prolonged and increasingly bloody war was waning, especially in Maryland and parts of Indiana and Illinois. Massive riots against the draft occurred in New York. While the president's Northern constituency would support a war to uphold the Union, it seemed that the people would not support huge losses of its sons and its wealth to free the slaves of the United States.

The Confederate States sent ambassadors to Britain and France seeking diplomatic recognition. Southern politicians believed that international recognition would give their

This photograph of Grant was taken in 1865 and shows him with the rank of lieutenant general, a rank held previously only by George Washington.

ANTIETAM NATIONAL BATTLEFIELD

This battle fought on September 17, 1862, marked the end of first Confederate invasion of the North. It is remembered as one of the costliest battles of the war—more than 23,000 men were killed, wounded, or missing after just a single day of fighting. Today, the site (map reference 4) in Maryland features a visitor center and numerous education programs. Visitors can take a self-guided tour of the battlefield or enjoy a variety of outdoor activities.

Nearly 180,000 black men served in the Union armed forces during the Civil War as is exemplified in this portrait of a cavalry soldier.

secession a legal, economic, and—just possibly—military boost. Ties with Britain were strong because the mills of that nation had a voracious appetite for Southern cotton. Recognition by Britain of the South as a separate state cou have sealed the North's fate. The British, however, waited see how the fall offensives would work out.

This period is often called the "high tide of the Confederacy." Confederate armies initiated attacks on three fronts: Mississippi, Kentucky, and Maryland. Robert E. Lee encountered McClellan's army at Antietam, Maryland, on September 17, 1862. That battle is remembered as the single bloodiest day of the Civil War, resulting in more than twenty-three thousand casualties among the young men who fought there. The Southern army was turned back. Despite horrific casualties, Northern politicians and army officers declared it a Union victory. Indeed, except for McClellan's timid battle tactics and the arrival of Southern reinforcements at a critical moment, Lee's army might very well have been destroyed

Antietam provided Lincoln the "victory" he needed to mo forward with freeing the slaves. On September 22, 1862, he issued the Emancipation Proclamation, which said that on January 1, 1863, slaves in rebelling states were to be set fre Laughed at in the South, where the president was powerles to enforce it, the proclamation was not popular in the Nort either. In addition, it did not apply to the border states— Delaware, Kentucky, Maryland, and Missouri—which had not seceded but had strong Southern sympathies.

Nevertheless, Lincoln's proclamation allowed Northern black men to become warriors in their own cause. By the end of the Civil War, 180,000 blacks, including Northerne and free blacks and newly freed slaves from the South, ha served in the Union army and navy. Many thousands mo worked as laborers for the army.

In his autobiography, Ulysses S. Grant noted that blac soldiers, former slaves with only sixteen days training, performed well during their first engagement at Milliken Bend, Louisiana, June 7, 1863. Assaulted by a larger Confederate force, the men of the First Mississippi (Afric Descent) fought hand-to-hand with Southerners.

rom Corinth to Vicksburg

hen Corinth fell, the Union troops in the West seemed ised to expand on their victory, but General Halleck was erly cautious and broke up his army into forces of cupation. He sent General Buell north to Chattanooga, nnessee, ordering him to rebuild rail links as he went. hen Halleck went to Washington in July, Grant and Buell came independent commanders, and it was their armies at took the force of Confederate attacks on Corinth, ississippi, and Perryville, Kentucky.

Buell held the Confederates at Perryville on October 8, d Grant defeated Earl Van Dorn's army at Corinth, forcing to retreat to central Mississippi. After this latest victory, ant was free to attack the bulwark of Confederate defenses the West: the fortress at Vicksburg, Mississippi, on the ississippi River. The citadel was well defended, however, th twenty-nine heavy cannons sitting on top of 200-foot 1-meters) bluffs. Even Farragut's naval guns could not und the fortress into submission. On those fortified ights, the rebels seemed—and felt—invincible.

"Whistling Dick"—one of the Confederate cannon that defended Vicksburg, on July 4, 1863

CHAPTER 5

VICTORIES AT VICKSBURG AND GETTYSBURG

In October 1862, shortly after Lincoln delivered the Emancipation Proclamation, Grant began his efforts to capture Vicksburg. His army of some forty thousand men (only half his total forces; the rest were needed for occupation) moved first toward Jackson, the capital of Mississippi. Meanwhile, his able lieutenant, William T. Sherman, gathered forces in Memphis with the idea of moving downriver and attacking Confederate forces under Pemberton and Van Dorn from two directions.

Things went wrong almost immediately: Grant was halted when Van Dorn captured the major Union supply base at Holly Springs, Mississippi and Sherman was defeated by Pemberton. To compound the problems, General John A. McClernand had been given permission to raise troops in the area and attack Vicksburg. McClernand arrived on the scene on January 2 and took command of

The Siege of Vicksburg by Union 13, 15, and 17 Corps. Grant is at bottom right.

This statue guards the base of the the Wisconsin State Memorial, one of many memorials in the Vicksburg National Military Park. The monument includes a granite column upon which sits a bronze statue of "Old Abe," the war eagle and mascot of the Eighth Wisconsin Infantry.

herman's forces, attacking and taking Fort Hindman. They uld do little against the well-sited defenses of Vicksburg.

Grant arrived outside Vicksburg at the end of January id took control, setting up his headquarters at Milliken's 2nd. He had some sixty-thousand men and organized em into three corps under McClernand, McPherson, and herman. He knew he was on the wrong side of Vicksburg, hich had strong defenses on the high ground to the north. e had always intended attacking from the east but feared e political repercussions that would follow if he moved vay from the city.

For two months, he tried to find a way around to the st, even digging a canal across the DeSoto Peninsula front of the city. In the end, he came up with a bold an. Admiral David Porter would run the gauntlet of the cksburg batteries to get his naval force downriver to ard Times Landing, while the army marched to meet em. From there, the navy would ferry the troops across e river. To hide this movement, Sherman would attack

FREDERICKSBURG AND SPOTSYLVANIA NATIONAL MILITARY PARK

Chancellorsville, Fredericksburg, The Wilderness, Spotsylvania—battlefields that will be remembered by generations of Americans—are commemorated by this northern Virginia park (map reference 14) that covers what some have called the bloodiest soil in the United States. Roughly one hundred thousand men were killed or wounded in fighting on these battlefields. The park's 8,000-plus acres (3,238 ha) include museums, visitor centers, cemeteries, walking paths, and monuments to soldiers and to famous General Thomas "Stonewall" Jackson.

These upturned cannons were recovered from the battlefield and serve as memorial obelisks among the fifteen thousand Union soldiers buried in the Fredericksburg and Spotsylvania National Military Park.

the northern heights. It was a gamble: If the plan failed, Porter's force would be on the wrong side of the city and would be cut to pieces if it attempted to go back upriver, past the batteries again.

On the night of April 16, Porter made his move. The Confederates quickly realized what was happening, but Porter's fleet made it through with only minor casualties. It then met up with the army—some forty-three thousand men—at Hard Times. They crossed the river, and Grant moved toward his original target, Jackson, the Mississippi state capital, which he captured on May 14. Two days late

e turned west and traveled along the Vicksburg and
ackson Railroad, positioning his troops to surround
icksburg's eastern defenses and cutting off the city from
e rest of the world.

The siege of Vicksburg took forty-eight days of hard
helling. In Vicksburg, the population was starving, and
onfederate General Pemberton finally surrendered on
ly 4, 1863. Grant had gained control of the mighty
ississippi River supply line, which was now in Union
ntrol all the way to the sea.

ettysburg

the East, the Army of the Potomac had changed
mmanders yet again. Burnside, who had taken over from
cClellan in November, was himself relieved of command
December when Joseph "Fighting Joe" Hooker took over.
ooker's army was severely beaten at Chancellorsville,
rginia, on May 1, 1863. The fighting at Chancellorsville
d Fredericksburg, Virginia, lost twenty thousand Union
es, and Hooker lost his job soon after to Major General
eorge Gordon Meade. Lee also lost his most able
mmander: Stonewall Jackson was mistakenly
ot by his own troops and died from his wounds.

After two years of war, it was apparent that Confederate
pplies were running out. Reinforcements were slow to
me, and Lee's troops were often hungry. Thousands

Grant was a renowned
horseman. His most
famous horse was
Cincinnati (*above*). At 17
hands [68 inches (1.7 m)]
high and very fast,
Cincinnati was an ideal
battle charger and served
Grant well until the end of
the war. Grant is supposed
to have refused an offer of
$10,000 for Cincinnati and
rarely allowed anyone else
to ride him. The only
exceptions were his
friends President Lincoln
and Admiral Daniel
Ammen. When Grant
was president, Cincinnati
lived in the White House
stables. Cincinnati
eventually died at
Admiral Ammen's farm
in Maryland in 1878.

An 1887 print showing
action during the battle
of Gettysburg

Reenactors at Gettysburg. The battle had a major effect on the war and has since become a metaphor for the titanic struggle between two brave and tenacious enemies.

marched and fought barefoot and in rags. They relied on taking clothing, weapons, and ammunition from captured Union soldiers. The time had come, Lee decided, to deal a blow to Northern armies on their home turf, perhaps driving a stake into the Union's will to fight. A successful offensive might settle the conflict. With the grudging support of the Confederate war department and politician in Richmond, Lee took the war north.

Lee's army swarmed north only one month after his victor at Chancellorsville. Meade had only recently taken charge, but he managed to stay between the Confederates and Washington. The ultimate collision of the armies—seventy-five thousand Southerners against ninety-five thousand Northerners—took place at a small town in Pennsylvania called Gettysburg during the first three days of July 1863.

Union and Confederate forces faced one another across relatively open ground, broken here and there by fences, cornfields, and small hills. The North occupied high grour east of the town, and the South attacked those positions. Days of murderous artillery shelling and hand-to-hand fighting followed on Cemetery Ridge, in the Devil's Den, and atop Little Round Top.

On July 3, having attacked both the Union right and left flanks unsuccessfully, Lee decided the center must be weak. Eighteen thousand men stood and walked uphill toward the waiting Union guns. They were decimated.

Statue of a soldier at Gettysburg National Military Park

Lee's army was beaten, and that night it began to retreat to Virginia. Losses to the Southern army were estimated at between twenty and twenty-eight thousand men. This was an irreplaceable number for the Confederacy, which soon began drafting teenagers and old men. The Northern states were jubilant, even though twenty-three thousand of their own soldiers had been killed or wounded in the battle.

Vicksburg: The Greater Victory?

Today, Gettysburg is seen as a pivotal moment in the history of the Civil War and as a pivotal moment in American consciousness. Before Gettysburg, it seemed that the South *might* win; afterward, everything seemed different. Thousands flock to the battlefield each year to reenact the battle, to remember the heroism of the attacking Confederates and the steadfastness of the Union forces. If people today know the name of one Civil War battle, it is likely to be Gettysburg.

Just days after the victory, newspapers announced that Vicksburg had fallen to Ulysses S. Grant. At the time, few would have recognized it as a greater victory than Gettysburg, but in many ways it was. The Confederates surrendered thirty thousand men, and, within a few days, the Mississippi River was in Union hands all the way to the sea. Strategically, the loss of Vicksburg and the river split the Confederate territories in two. Perhaps most important of all, the victory showed Grant's worth.

Together, the successes at Vicksburg and Gettysburg were welcome news to a Union that had sacrificed so much and suffered so many defeats. Despite terrible losses to come, the North would grit its teeth and complete what needed to be done to reunite the United States. After these victories, any realistic hope died that foreign powers would recognize or assist the seceding states.

Even though the Confederate States maintained armies in the field for two more years, the events of July 1863 put an end to serious thoughts of Southern victory. The man most responsible for directing the war to its end would be Ulysses S. Grant. When General Rosecrans's Army of the Cumberland was defeated at Chickamauga, Georgia on September 19–20, Lincoln and Halleck agreed to make Grant overall commander of Union armies in the West. Within six months, Grant would be commander in chief of all the Union armies.

CHAPTER 6
GRANT IN CHARGE

The battle on the slopes of Lookout Mountain, during the siege of Chattanooga, November 24, 1863.

The battle of Gettysburg marked the midway point in a long and miserable war that took its toll on both sides. Much vicious fighting remained, although from Gettysburg onward, the Union mostly marched from victory to victory.

After Gettysburg, it seemed that the armies of the East and their commanders were exhausted. That was certainly true of Lee's Confederates, and Lincoln was disappointed that Meade failed to take advantage of his victory.

In the West, the Union victory at Vicksburg did not force the Confederate army to collapse. In fact, the opposite was true. During the siege of Vicksburg, the other significant Union force in the West, William S. Rosecrans's Army of the Cumberland, had marched toward the important railroad center of Chattanooga, Tennessee, and forced the Confederate Army of Tennessee under Braxton Bragg to fall back. Rosecrans thought he had the Confederates on the run, but he was wrong. The two armies met on September 19–20 at Chickamauga Creek, Georgia, and fought an enormous and bloody battle in difficult terrain. At Chickamauga, the forest and underbrush were thick, and whole regiments and divisions—on both sides of the battle—lost contact with their commanders. The result was a very costly victory for Confederate General Bragg, who held the field when

osecrans fled. Only General George Thomas saved
e day for the Union, rallying his men long enough
r reinforcements to arrive. His action earned him the
ickname "Rock of Chickamauga." Losses were high—
ghteen thousand Confederates and sixteen thousand
nion men—and this may explain in part why Bragg
d not follow up the victory. Rosecrans's defeated army
aggered into Chattanooga.

Lincoln reacted immediately to Rosecrans's failure at
hickamauga and relieved him of his command of the
rmy of the Cumberland. The president turned to Grant
d put him in charge of all the Union armies in the West.
rant immediately replaced Rosecrans with Thomas and
ade for Chattanooga, arriving in the city on October 23.

The situation looked desperate. Bragg's army commanded
e heights above the city—Missionary Ridge and Lookout
ountain—and had cut off the Union's supply line—the
nnessee River—that ran below. The Union forces were
tnumbered almost two to one and could have been
pected to lack morale.

Within days, the Union situation improved. First, Grant
stored his supply lines. General "Baldy" Smith secured a
ossing over the Tennessee River that allowed supplies to
ach the city. That day, Hooker and his corps of sixteen
ousand arrived. Grant's forces were further boosted when
erman arrived with twenty thousand men. At the same
ne, a quarrel between two Confederate generals led to one
them taking fifteen thousand men off to east Tennessee.
hen Grant made his move on November 23, his force
seventy thousand faced forty thousand Confederates.

A sketch by Alfred Waud of the battle of Chickamauga on September 21, 1863. The success for the Confederates would lead President Lincoln to put Grant in charge of all Union forces in the West. Waud (1828–1891) was one of the special artists sent out by *Harper's Weekly* to cover the war.

General Grant receiving his commission as lieutenant general from President Lincoln in an illustration from *Harper's Weekly* in 1864. At last Lincoln had found the general who would win the war.

Grant's plan at Chattanooga was deceptively simple. There would be diversionary attacks on the left of Bragg's line—Lookout Mountain—by Hooker and in the center by Thomas. Sherman's assault on the north of Missionary Ridge would be the main thrust.

As is so often the case in battle, things did not go according to plan. Sherman's thrust was held up, and Thomas's diversionary attack ended with his troops storming Missionary Ridge in one of the epic assaults of the war. The Union army did force the Confederate army to retreat into Georgia, and the siege of Chattanooga was lifted.

Grant Takes Command

By the winter of 1863–64, Lincoln was through with the overly cautious Meade. He offered the command of his armies to the one man who seemed capable of leading the Union to victory: Ulysses S. Grant. Grant accepted and was promoted lieutenant general—a rank previously held only by George Washington. He arrived in Washington on March 8, 1864. Almost immediately, in early May, he moved the Army of the Potomac south. Few could have realized that the Civil War—almost three years old—had less than one year to run.

Grant's overall strategy was based on three significant factors:

• That the difference between his army and that of Lee's was resources. With a population twice that of the eleven seceding states, Grant's supply of men and materiel was greater, whereas every Southern casualty brought the Confederacy closer to its end. Grant's strategy would be to attack. In spite of winning or losing individual battles, his army would advance, move forward, and keep up the pressure. He would take men away from garrison duty to increase the size of his fighting forces, and Lincoln would supply more men through the February 1, 1864 draft, which called for five hundred thousand men.

• That warfare was inherently cruel and inhumane. In th face of repeating rifles and powerful high explosives, the

CIVIL WAR MEDICINE

By today's standards, Civil War medicine was primitive. Thousands of men died from disease and infection. With no licensing boards, the eleven thousand Northern and three thousand Southern doctors often worked with a minimum of training and little or no surgical experience.

Imagine the scene. Suddenly inundated with hundreds of bleeding, groaning, and screaming men, field surgeons practiced "triage." They first helped those who could be saved and lay aside those whose wounds—to the head or body—were invariably death sentences. Chloroform numbed wounded men to the pain, but supplies in the South soon ran out. Instruments were dropped in the dirt, picked up, wiped off on a surgeon's apron, and immediately used again. Flies and rats were everywhere. Badly wounded soldiers might lie for days on the battlefield until they bled to death, died of exposure and shock, or were perhaps killed by dogs and vultures.

Musket balls were huge, and soft lead minie balls, often with cylindrical bodies, became larger when they hit because they flattened or "mushroomed." The Harper's Ferry and Springfield Armories produced about sixty thousand Model 1855 U.S. Percussion Rifle-Muskets that fired 58-caliber minie balls. These measured more than one-half inch (1 cm) in diameter.

If a ball struck the bone in a soldier's arm or leg—and 70 percent of recorded wounds were to the limbs—a surgeon had little choice but to amputate. A good surgeon could amputate a limb in ten minutes, and gruesome mounds of body parts piled up near the field surgeon's tent.

Hit in the leg by two projectiles, 5 inches (12 cm) of General John Bell Hood's upper thigh bone were shattered. Hip amputations, such as that performed on Hood, had an astonishing mortality rate of 83 percent. When he was shipped home, they sent the leg with him, expecting him to die, but he did not. Arm amputations, like the one that eventually resulted in the death of Stonewall Jackson, had a 24 percent mortality rate.

**Reenactors give a graphic representation of Civil War surgeons.
In front of them is an array of surgical equipment from the period.**

days of dashing cavaliers and gentlemanly duels were over. Gone were the days when lines of opposing soldiers stood to fire at one another at fifty yards. War had changed. During the Civil War, warfare demanded trenches and strongly fortified shelters.

• That his objective was to destroy the Confederate armies not to capture Richmond or occupy territory. Destroying rebel armies meant devastating their system of supply and support. This required making war on the civilian infrastructure that produced food, clothing, guns, and ammunition.

Grant's military strategy is shown on the map (*right*). Sherman, his most trusted lieutenant, was given command of the armies of the West—one hundred thousand men—and told to go after the Confederate forces of Joe Johnston. Grant himself was going after Lee, with General Franz Sigel attacking through the Shenandoah Valley and General Benjamin Butler's Army of the James on the offensive on the Yorktown Peninsula. The remaining theater, a minor one in the Southwest, saw an ineffectual offensive by General Banks.

Initially, Grant had planned to get rid of Meade and take over the Army of the Potomac but, after meeting the "Old

The battle of Franklin, on November 30, 1864, was between Confederate forces commanded by John Bell Hood and a Union corps under John M. Schofield. While the Union withdrew at Franklin, Hood lost so many men at this battle and subsequently at the battle of Nashville that he was not able to stop Sherman marching to Savannah, Georgia.

MINNESOTA • WISCONSIN • MICHIGAN • NEW YORK • Lake Ontario • Niagara Falls • Lowell • Syracuse • Albany • Boston • Rochester • Springfield • Hartford • MA • Providence • Buffalo • Lake Huron • Lansing • Madison • Milwaukee • Detroit • Erie • Lake Erie • Stamford • New Haven • CT • RI • Newark • New York • Waterloo • Cedar Rapids • Rockford • Chicago • Toledo • Cleveland • PENNSYLVANIA • Allentown • NJ • Trenton • IOWA • Davenport • Gary • Fort Wayne • Akron • Pittsburgh • Harrisburg • Philadelphia • Des Moines • Peoria • OHIO • Columbus • Dover • Springfield • ILLINOIS • INDIANA • Dayton • Baltimore • MD • DE • Annapolis • Indianapolis • Cincinnati • W. VIRGINIA (1863) • Saint Joseph • Terre Haute • Louisville • Frankfort • Charleston • VIRGINIA • Richmond • Virginia Beach • Kansas City • Saint Louis • Lexington • Lynchburg • Norfolk • Jefferson City • Missouri R. • Evansville • Ohio R. • KENTUCKY • Danville • MISSOURI • Springfield • Clarksville • Nashville • Knoxville • Greensboro • N. CAROLINA • Raleigh • TERRITORY • Fort Smith • Memphis • Jackson • Murfreesboro • Chattanooga • Charlotte • Little Rock • TENNESSEE • Decatur • Columbia • Wilmington • ARKANSAS • Birmingham • Atlanta • S. CAROLINA • Macon • Augusta • Monroe • Montgomery • Columbus • Charleston • Shreveport • Jackson • ALABAMA • GEORGIA • Savannah • EXAS • MISSISSIPPI • Mobile • Jacksonville • Baton Rouge • Pensacola • Tallahassee • LOUISIANA • FLORIDA • uston • New Orleans • Orlando • Sarasota

SIGEL
GRANT
BUTLER
SHERMAN
BANKS

Atlantic Ocean

AREA UNDER FEDERAL CONTROL
FEDERAL NAVAL BLOCKADE
AREA UNDER CONFEDERATE CONTROL
AREA ISOLATED FROM DIRECT CONFEDERATE CONTROL

apping Turtle," decided not to do so. He would travel with
e army like an admiral in his flagship. On May 4, Grant
ossed the Rapidan, and the plan was put into action.

The strategy was a good one and, eventually, would
rk, but as spring became summer, the Union did not seem
be making spectacular headway. In the West, Sherman's
emy, General Joe Johnston, performed brilliantly, giving
ground rather than men and not allowing Sherman the
tched battle he knew the Confederates would lose.

erman had three armies—Thomas's Army of the
mberland (sixty thousand men), McPherson's Army of
nnessee (thirty thousand men), and Schofield's Army of
e Ohio (seventeen thousand men). Johnston had forty-five
ousand men, later reinforced to sixty thousand.

Grant's strategy to end the war was based on head-on confrontation, with Sherman attacking Joe Johnston in the West and the Eastern Union armies going for Lee. It was a strategy that would work, but at great cost.

Then, as so often in war, politics played its part. Jefferson Davis, who could not see the brilliance of Johnston, replaced him with John Bell Hood. Hood attacked Sherman's forces and lost, and attacked again, losing thousands of irreplaceable troops and supplies in each battle. On September 2, 1864, Sherman's forces entered Atlanta, Georgia, and destroyed Hood's army at Franklin and Nashville. Then Sherman cut loose from his extended supply and communications lines and, with sixty thousand veteran soldiers, marched southeast toward Savannah, Georgia, and the Atlantic coast. Along the way, he destroyed plantations, mills, and warehouses; he burned everything that could support the rebellion. Marching without baggage or supply columns, his troops took what they needed wherever they found it. On December 23, 1864, Sherman arrived in Savannah and looked out upon the Atlantic Ocean.

The campaign through Georgia strangled the seceding states, cutting rail and telegraph connections and preventing supplies from flowing north to Lee's embattled Virginia army. Sherman had waged total war. In the wake of its march to the sea, however, his army sowed the seeds of a century of hatred.

An 1893 etching showing Sherman during his "march to the sea."

CHAPTER 7
BATTLING TOWARD THE END

Earlier, in the spring of 1864, Grant had faced stiff resistance every step of the way when he pushed his army into Virginia. May 1864 saw some of the bloodiest battles of the war: a second battle at The Wilderness (total casualties of more than twenty-five thousand); at Spotsylvania, Virginia (more than twenty-seven thousand casualties); and at Cold Harbor, Virginia (eighty-five hundred casualties). During May, the South emerged with more clear victories; furthermore, the Union suffered around fifty-two thousand casualties compared to about thirty-three thousand for the Confederates. Nonetheless, the losses were not as damaging to the larger Union forces as they were to the shrinking Southern army. Realizing this, Robert E. Lee had his troops fall back and build earthen fortifications around Petersburg, Virginia, just outside Richmond. The Union army dug in facing it. Grant's strategy was to engage in nonstop siege warfare: entrench, attack, and bombard.

By this time, death had crept into every home in the nation. Although he was eventually victorious, Grant was attacked in the Northern press as a drunk and a butcher. Lincoln, however, never lost faith in his brilliant military leader.

Grant had many failings, but timidity while in command of his army was not one of them. One of his generals presented a plan at Petersburg to use miners (called "sappers") to undermine the Confederate trenches and fortified earthworks. The miners were certain they could set off an enormous explosion beneath the Southerners. Then, waiting Union troops could rush through the gap, overwhelm the stunned rebels, and perhaps bring an end to the war.

General Grant (*standing front*) and his staff in Cold Harbor, Virginia, June 11 or 12, 1864. Photograph taken by Mathew B. Brady.

A sketch made of the Petersburg Crater from the Union side.

The Union moved forward with the plan, and the explosion opened an enormous pit beneath the Confederate line. The blast killed, wounded, and buried scores of rebels. Union troops now charged forward, only to discover that they were trapped in a 30-foot (9-m) hole and could not get out. No one had thought to bring scaling ladders. The sides of the crater were steep; the soil was loose and sandy. The men were trapped and could not climb out. Worse, driven by their officers, the troops behind them pushed forward relentlessly. Men packed in so tight that they could not raise their arms. Soon, the stunned Confederates rallied, bringing fresh men to the edge of the great hole. Soldiers who managed to climb out fought viciously, stabbing

ith their bayonets and swinging
heir muskets like clubs. Those
ft in the hole were shot down
r speared by bayonets.

What is now known as the
attle of the Crater was a
ebacle. More than 6,000 men
ere killed and wounded that
ay, the Union army losing most
that total. The next morning,
oth sides called a truce. As
nion and Confederate bands
ayed, men buried the dead and
covered the wounded. General
mbrose Burnside, who was
sponsible for the fiasco, was
lieved of duty. The Union army,
hich had allowed a great plan
fail at the cost of great pain
d suffering to those involved,

Grant (*at left leaning over*)
examining a map with
his staff at Massaponax
Church, his temporary
headquarters in Virginia,
on May 21, 1864.

ttled into a grueling eight months of siege warfare.
From 1864 until 1865, the siege meant almost daily
mbardments. Northern units attacked, searching for
eak points in the Confederate defenses. The Confederates
unterattacked. Grant patiently extended his lines,
nowing that Sherman's march to the sea in Georgia, the
rangling naval blockade, and the destruction of Southern
mies elsewhere meant that sooner, rather than later, he
uld overwhelm Lee's army.
By the beginning of 1865, the situation of the Army
Northern Virginia was precarious. Food, clothing, and
mmunition were nonexistent. Desertions were increasing,
d illnesses such as dysentery and pneumonia decimated
e ranks. The civilian populace suffered likewise.
Lee understood that he could no longer defend the
onfederate capital. If his army continued to occupy its
enches and fortifications, it would be slowly ground down
d then suddenly overwhelmed. He decided to withdraw
d sacrifice the capital to save his army—already less than
lf the size of Grant's. Perhaps he could join forces with the

army in North Carolina and defeat Sherman before rallying to fight Grant again. To disengage his forces, he needed to loosen the Union grip on Petersburg. As a diversion, he sent John B. Gordon to attack Fort Stedman on March 25.

The attack failed. Grant realized what Lee was trying to do and ordered an advance on all fronts. Urging Lee to fight on, the Confederate government fled, and on April 3, 1865, Grant's troops occupied Richmond. The following day, Abraham Lincoln visited the rebel capital. Barely 110 miles (177 km) from Washington, Richmond had tantalized him and his armies for four years.

Small, bloody battles followed as Grant hounded the retreating Confederates, whose numbers dwindled with every action. By the time Lee reached Appomattox, Virginia, he had about thirteen thousand men.

On April 7, Grant realized he was close to victory. He spent the night at the same hotel in Farmville where Lee had slept the previous night. There, the general who abhorred "sport hunting," who had become ill watching a bullfight in Mexico, but who demanded "unconditional surrender" and then offered compassionate, even generous terms when the rebels were firmly within his grasp, wrote the following message to Lee: "The results of the last week must convince you of the hopelessness of further resistance. I feel that is so, and regard it as my duty to shift the responsibility of any further effusion of blood, by asking of you the surrender of that portion of the Confederate States army known as the Army of Northern Virginia."

Receiving Grant's note, Lee allowed his generals to voice their opinions. Unanimously, they still wanted to fight. Accordingly, Lee sent troops forward to battle, but they were defeated. Watching that fight, Lee realized his cause was lost.

"There is nothing left me but to go see General Grant," he said, "and I had rather die a thousand deaths."

Lee surrendered the next day, April 9, 1865, in a private home at Appomattox Court House, Virginia. A handsome and engaging man, Lee represented the ruling aristocracy of the Southern states by wearing his finest uniform, with a bright sash and a sword whose hilt was trimmed in gold.

A nineteenth-century view of Appomattox Court House.

APPOMATTOX COURT HOUSE NATIONAL HISTORIC PARK

On April 9, 1865, Robert E. Lee surrendered to Ulysses S. Grant at the private McLean home at this site. Today in this park (map reference 5), the visitor's center/museum and the McLean house are open year-round; twenty-seven original nineteenth-century buildings survive in the park.

rant, a modest and unimposing figure, represented the orthern states by riding to the meeting in his usual, ud-spattered coat.

The two men signed an agreement for Lee's soldiers to lay own their arms, and at 3 p.m., four years after the war egan, it was over. President Davis wanted the Confederate rmies to disperse and fight a guerrilla war, but the desperate onfederate Army of Tennessee under Joe Johnston— elatedly brought out of retirement by Lee—soon surrendered Sherman in North Carolina. Sherman offered terms that ere even more generous than those made by Grant to Lee.

An etching of the capitulation and surrender of Lee and his army at Appomattox on April 9, 1865

CHAPTER 8
FROM GENERAL TO PRESIDENT

I n a larger sense, the Civil War was not settled on the battlefields. Half a million families mourned loved one killed during the fighting. A million men lost arms and legs. The Southern states were ruined, the Northern state were deeply in debt, and four million former slaves needed to be integrated as citizens into the reconstituted Union.

Lincoln might have been able to pull the pieces together. He had urged the people of the North to look on the rebels as wayward brothers, not defeated foes. His agenda promoted reconciliation and forgiveness. However, five days after Lee's army lay down its arms and marched into history, Lincoln attended Ford's Theatre with his wife, Mary. At 10:15 p.m., an actor with Confederate sympathies, John Wilkes Booth, slipped behind Lincoln and shot him in the head. The president died the next morning.

Lincoln's death inflamed the Northern states, and a group of Republican politicians known as "Radicals" promoted harsh policies for the "reconstruction" of the South. Initially, former Confederate officers were barred from public office. Confederate states were forced to reapply for statehood with new constitutions, and a condition for statehood was ratification of the constitutional amendments that abolished slavery, gave the exslaves citizenship, and gave them the right to vote.

These were the days of the "carpetbaggers," so-called because they traveled light, carrying soft-sided luggage made from material that resembled carpeting. Usually, these were Northerners who expected to profit from the desperation of the Southerners, both white and black, and so carpetbagger became a nasty name for a meddling outsider. Adding insult to injury from the white

A "broadside" (wanted poster) after Lincoln's assassination.

outherners' point of view, many federal troops sent to ey points of occupation were black soldiers. In response, outherners formed a secret society called the Ku Klux lan, which was dedicated to white supremacy. The lan, or KKK, specialized in terrorizing black people nd their supporters, burning their schools, churches, nd businesses, and murdering men and women alike often by hanging, called lynching).

Thousands of black families emigrated because of the error, because of the lack of real federal protection, and ecause there was no way for the former slaves to earn a ving except as tenants or sharecroppers for their former asters who still owned the land. Perhaps the most nfortunate legacy of the war was that U.S. politicians oon forgot their promises to the new black citizens. s a consequence, racism is a legacy of the Civil War and as not yet disappeared from the heart of the United States.

rant for President

rant's journey after the war was utterly different from is struggle with poverty, shabby clothing, and menial jobs n the late 1850s. He was a hero, and even as Andrew ohnson, a Tennessee Democrat, completed Lincoln's term f office, the Republican Party nominated Grant for the residency. He refused to campaign—he hated giving peeches—but he was elected anyway. It is said that the

FORD'S THEATER NATIONAL HISTORIC SITE

The theater, (map reference 10) where Lincoln was shot by John Wilkes Booth, and Petersen's boarding house across the street, in which he died, have been preserved for all to visit today. Ford's is still a working theater, featuring live performances. It is open daily year-round and features hourly talks that provide the fascinating story of the theater and the tragic events that make it so famous.

This Mathew Brady photograph of the ruins of Secession Hall, Charleston, South Carolina, sums up the country's immediate postwar problems.

Grant delivers his inauguration speech on the East Portico of the U.S. Capitol on March 4, 1873, at the start of his second term in office.

nation saw him as an honest, straightforward soldier who would end the political bickering and under whom life could return to normal.

Unfortunately, without political experience, Grant soon foundered, particularly after his faithful chief of staff, John Rawlins, died in 1869. His administration was thoroughly scandal ridden, as shown dramatically on Black Friday, September 24, 1869, when two New York stock gamblers, Jay Gould and Jim Fisk, aided by people high up in the government, almost cornered the market in gold.

Grant was reelected by an even wider margin in 1872, and the scandals continued. The Credit Mobilier Company diverted profits from Union Pacific into directors' pockets and congressmen were paid off to stop their intervention. The President's private secretary, General Orville E. Babcock, was involved in a whiskey ring that defrauded the government of taxes. Even though Grant himself did not benefit, there was evidence that he understood and was unable or unwilling to manage the strong personalitie and hidden agendas of Washington politics.

Nevertheless, there were successes. In foreign affairs in particular, Grant and his excellent secretary of state, Hamilton Fish, were able to solve a problem with Great Britain caused by the actions of the C.S.S. *Alabama*. This ironclad, with a Confederate captain and British crew, had attacked and destroyed sixty-four Union vessels before being sunk off Cherbourg, France, by U.S.S. *Kearsage*. Grant insisted on a peaceful approach to solve the problem and succeeded. In the 1871 Treaty of Washington, Britain agreed to pay the U.S. $15.5 million in compensation.

After eight years in high office, Grant retired. He took Julia on an amazing two-year, round-the-world vacation. Kings gave them banquets. Queens talked with Julia. In dozens of nations, massive crowds lined the streets just to get a glimpse of America's great general.

Home at last, Grant started a brokerage business in New York City. With his usual business luck, however, it failed, leaving his family penniless. His trusted partner had embezzled the company's assets, including Grant's life savings.

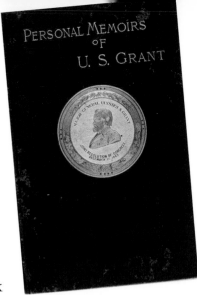

This 1870s photo taken in New Jersey shows, from left to right: Henry (butler), Julia Grant (wife), Grant himself, Nellie (daughter), Ferdinand (valet), Jesse (son), U.S. Grant, Jr. (son, known as "Buck"), and Willie Coles, a friend of Jesse's.

Grant's funeral procession on August 8, 1885, seen at Fifth Avenue and Fifty-eighth Street, New York City

Desperate, Grant wrote his autobiography, and his friend Mark Twain (born Samuel Clemens) edited and published it. During the writing, Grant struggled with throat cancer; the illness made it difficult to speak. He was ill and penniless when Congress stepped in. He had given up his military rank when he became president. Congress now restored it, ensuring that he and his dependents would receive a military pension.

1897 lithograph by Currier and Ives of Grant's tomb

GENERAL GRANT NATIONAL MEMORIAL

Grant's Tomb—and that of his wife, Julia Dent Grant—is located in Manhattan in the heart of New York City (map reference 15). Grant died in Mount McGregor, New York, on July 23, 1885, and was laid to rest in the tomb on August 8, 1885. Today, park rangers offer guided tours and programs at the memorial, and costumed interpreters introduce visitors to the former president and Civil War hero and his many accomplishments.

Grant completed his autobiography a few days before he died. The two-volume set was an immediate bestseller.

Grant, looking frail and suffering from cancer, writing his memoirs at Mt. McGregor, June 27, 1885

The Verdict of History

Grant was a complicated man who aroused complicated emotions. He had many critics—particularly of his drinking and the scandals that accompanied his administration. Grant's presidency was, by every account, corrupt. Many military historians have suggested that Lee was a better general. The verdict of history, however, is generous to the general. He is not accused of personal corruption. Indeed, his poverty at the end of his life was not the condition of a corrupt man. It was simply the fault of trusting the wrong people. He was, undoubtedly, a great general, whether he was the best general of the war or not. His contemporaries certainly thought him so. The common soldiery said of him, "Ulysses don't scare worth a damn." Lincoln was his enthusiastic supporter. General William T. Sherman called him "the greatest soldier of our time" General Philip Sheridan said, "When his military history is analyzed after the lapse of years, it will show, even more clearly than now, he was the steadfast center about and on which everything else turned.

The public remembered him generously, too. Twice, he became president. After his death, people from all over the world donated more than $600,000 to pay for the construction of his tomb—the largest public fundraising effort ever at that time. More than one million people watched the parade and dedication ceremony of the tomb on April 27, 1897, remembering his journey from the western periphery of the Civil War to Appomattox, from disgraced soldier to victorious general, from schoolboy to president.

U.S. GRANT HOME STATE HISTORIC SITE

From the end of the Civil War to the beginning of his presidency, Grant lived in a beautiful home given to him by the appreciative citizens of Galena, Illinois—the town in which he lived and worked as a lowly clerk prior to the war. The Grant family eventually gave the property to the State of Illinois (map reference 31). Today the home looks much the same as it did when Grant left for the White House in 1868.

Places to Visit and Research

Many sites crucial to Ulysses S. Grant's life and the Civil War can be researched on line or visited. Below is a list, in alphabetical order, of many Civil War museums, parks, and protected sites along with their addresses, telephone numbers, and Web sites. Places described in the sidebars that accompany the main text have a page reference. The green dots on the map on page 59 represent sites described in the sidebars; red dots represent sites that are also important to the story of Grant and the Civil War.

1 The Abraham Lincoln Presidential Library and Museum
112 N. Sixth Street, Springfield, IL 62701. (217) 558-8882. www.alplm.org
This new museum and library features interactive exhibits that tell the story of Lincoln's life and times.

2 African American Civil War Memorial
900 Ohio Ave. Drive SW, Washington, D.C. 20024. (202) 426-6841. www.nps.gov/afam
More than 209,000 members of the USCT (U.S. Colored Troops) fought in Union blue. This site is dedicated to them.

3 Andersonville National Historic Site
496 Cemetery Road, Andersonville, GA 31711. (229) 924-0343. www.nps.gov/ande. See page 30.

4 Antietam National Battlefield and Cemetery
P.O. Box 158, Sharpsburg, MD 21782-0158. (301) 432-5124. www.nps.gov/anti. See page 32.

5 Appomattox Courthouse National Historic Park
Highway 24, P.O. Box 218, Appomattox, VA 24522 (434) 352-8987, ext. 26 www.nps.gov/apco. See page 51.

6 Atlanta Cyclorama and Civil War Museum
Grant Park, 800 Cherokee Avenue S.E., Atlanta, GA 30315. (404) 624-1071/658-7625.

www.webguide.com/cyclorama.html
The story of the battle of Atlanta and historic Civil War locomotive Texas are at this museum in Grant Park.

7 Chickamauga and Chattanooga National Military Park
P.O. Box 2128, Fort Oglethorpe, GA 30742. (706) 866-9241. www.nps.gov/chch. See page 41.

8 Clara Barton National Historic Site
5801 Oxford Road, Glen Echo, MD 20812. (301) 492-6245. www.nps.gov/clba

9 Columbus-Belmont State Park
350 Park Road, Columbus, KY 42032-0009. (270) 677-2327. parks.ky.gov/stateparks/cb/index.htm. See page 21.

10 Ford's Theatre National Historic Site
511 10th Street NW, Washington, DC 20004. (202) 426-6924. www.nps.gov/foth. See page 53.

11 Fort Donelson National Battlefield and Cemetery
P.O. Box 434, Dover, TN 37058-0434. (931) 232-5348/5706. www.nps.gov/fodo. See page 27.

12 Fort Scott National Historic Site
P.O. Box 918, Fort Scott, KS 66701-0918. (620) 223-0310. www.nps.gov/fosc
Important mid-nineteenth century military installation with twenty historic structures.

13 Fort Sumter National Monument
1214 Middle Street, Sullivan's Island, SC 29482. (843) 883-3123. www.nps.gov/fosu. See page 12.

14 Fredericksburg and Spotsylvania National Military Park
120 Chatham Lane, Fredericksburg VA 22405-2508. (540) 373-6122. www.nps.gov/frsp. See page 36.

15 General Grant National Memorial
Riverside Drive and 122nd Street, New York, NY 10027. (202) 666-166 www.nps.gove/gegr. See page 56.

16 Gettysburg National Military Park
97 Taneytown Road, Gettysburg, PA 17325-2804. (717) 334-1124. www.nps.gov/gett. See page 39.

17 Harpers Ferry National Historic Park
P.O. Box 65, Harpers Ferry, WV 25425.(304) 535-6029. www.nps.gov/hafe. See page 19.

18 Hubbard House Underground Railroad Museu
P.O. Box 2666, Ashtabula, OH 44005-2666. (440) 964-8168 www.hubbardhouseugrrmuseum.o
Learn more about the secret sla route to freedom. Another site dedicated to the Railroad is the National Underground Railroad Museum, 115 E Third St., Maysville, KY 41056.

**Kennesaw Mountain
National Battlefield Park**
0 Kennesaw Mountain Drive,
Kennesaw, GA 30152. (770) 427-
86. www.nps.gov/kemo.
e page 44.

Lincoln Memorial
0 Ohio Drive SW, Washington,
C. 20024. (202) 426-6841.
ww.nps.gov/linc
he of the nation's most-
easured structures. The view
m the base of the Reflecting
ol and the Washington
onument is one every American
ould see.

**Manassas National
ttlefield Park**
521 Lee Highway, Manassas, VA
109-2005. (703) 361-133921.
ww.nps.gov/mana. See page 22.

**The Mariner's Museum—
SS Monitor Center**
0 Museum Drive, Newport News,
23606. (757) 596-2222.
ww.monitorcenter.org. See page 26.

**The Museum of the
nfederacy**
)1 E. Clay Street, Richmond, VA
219. (804) 649-1861.
ww.moc.org
e "White House of the
nfederacy" was preserved and
day includes a museum,
tifacts, library, visiting lecturers,
d tours.

**Olustee Battlefield Historic
ate Park**
). Box 40, Olustee, FL 32072.
6) 758-0400.
ww.floridastateparks.org/olustee
s park honors a February 1864
ttle in which the Union tried
d failed to cut Florida out of the
nfederacy. Three units of black
ion troops played a significant
e in the fighting.

**Petersburg National
ttlefield**
89 Hickory Hill Road,
ersburg, VA 23803-4721.

(804) 732-3531.www.nps.gov/pete.
See page 50.

**26 Richmond National
Battlefield Park**
3215 E Broad Street, Richmond, VA
23223. (804) 226-1981.
www.nps.gov/rich
**This park in Virginia's capital
includes eleven scattered units
covering 1,400 acres (570 ha).**

**27 Shiloh National Military
Park**
1055 Pittsburg Landing Road,
Shiloh, TN 38376. (731) 689-5696.
www.nps.gove/shil. See page 28.

**28 Smithsonian National
Museum of American History**
14th Street and Constitution
Avenue NW, Washington, D.C.
20001. (202) 633-1000.
americanhistory.si.edu
**The Smithsonian holds thousands
of photos, artifacts, books, maps,
and oral histories. Among the
many items on display is the
actual chair used by Grant during**

**the surrender ceremony at
Appomattox Court House.**

**29 The U.S. National Slavery
Museum**
1320 Central Park Blvd., Suite 251,
Fredericksburg, VA 22401.
(540) 548-8818. www.usnsm.org
**This new museum houses
exhibits, library, and interactive
learning experiences.**

**30 Ulysses S. Grant National
Historic Site**
7400 Grant Road, St. Louis, MO
63123. (314) 842-3298.
www.nps.gov/ulsg. See page 11.

**31 U.S. Grant Home State
Historic Site**
P.O. Box 333, Galena, IL 61036.
(815) 777-3310. www.granthome.com.
See page 57.

**32 Vicksburg National
Military Park**
3201 Clay Street, Vicksburg, MS
39183. (601) 636-0583.
www.nps.gov/vick. See page 35.

**This map shows the location of the places identified in the Places
to Visit and Research section. Those places shown in green are also
mentioned in sidebars.**

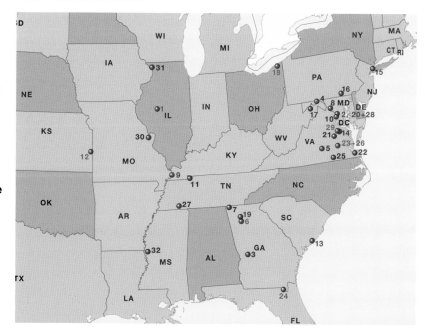

Time Line

1822
Grant is born at Point Pleasant, OH, April 27.

1843
Grant graduates from U.S. Military Academy. Posted to St. Louis.

1846–1847
War with Mexico

1848
Grant marries Julia.

1854
Grant leaves army, returns to St. Louis.

1859
John Brown's raid on Harpers Ferry, VA. Grant accepts clerkship in brothers' store.

1860
Lincoln elected president. South Carolina secedes.

1861
January Alabama, Florida, Georgia, Louisiana, and Mississippi secede.
February Texas secedes. Jefferson Davis inaugurated as president of the Confederacy.
April Attack on Fort Sumter, SC.
May Arkansas, North Carolina, Tennessee, and Virginia secede.
June Grant is appointed Colonel of Twenty-first Illinois Infantry.
August Grant promoted to brigadier general.

1862
February Grant takes Fort Henry and Fort Donelson.
April Battle of Shiloh, TN.
September Lincoln delivers Emancipation Proclamation.

1863
May Battle of Chancellorsville, VA.
July Battle of Gettysburg, PA. Grant takes Vicksburg. Appoints Sherman to drive toward Atlanta.
September Battle of Chickamauga, GA.
October Grant wins at Chattanooga, TN.

1864
March Grant becomes lieutenant general, head of all Union armies.
May Battles of Spotsylvania and The Wilderness.
June Battle of Cold Harbor. Grant begins siege of Petersburg.
September Sherman occupies Atlanta.
November Lincoln reelected. Sherman's "March to the Sea."

1865
January Thirteenth Amendment abolishes slavery.
April Petersburg falls. Grant occupies Richmond, VA. Lee surrenders at Appomattox, VA. Lincoln is assassinated. Andrew Johnson becomes president. Army of Tennessee surrenders to Sherman.

1866
Fourteenth Amendment guarantees citizenship to all born in U.S. Grant appointed four-star general, then secretary of war.

1868
Grant elected president; at forty-six, he is the youngest to hold the office.

1869
Fifteenth Amendment declares a person's righ[t] to vote cannot be denie[d] based on race, color, or previous condition as a slave.

1871
Treaty of Washington with Great Britain.

1872
Grant reelected president despite administration scandals.

1877
Grant leaves White House and opens business in New York. Federal troops withdraw from South.

1878–1879
Grant family makes around-the-world tour[.]

1884
Grant bankrupt as business partner embezzles money. Diagnosed with cance[r.] Begins writing memo[irs.]

1885
Completes memoirs, July 19. Grant dies, July 23.

Glossary

Abolitionist A person who called for the eradication of slavery.

Arsenal A place where guns and ammunition are manufactured and/or stored.

Blockade runner Small, fast ships used to evade Union naval vessels blockading Confederate ports.

Casualty Soldier or sailor removed from service by death, wounds, or sickness.

Civil war War between sections or regions within the same country.

Constitution Fundamental U.S. law. Developed by 1789, denied full citizenship to women and to people of color.

Cotton Soft, white hairs growing on seeds of the mallow family, used to make fabric. Together with tobacco formed the economic foundation of the Confederacy.

Draft (or conscription) Required enrollment for military service.

Ironclad A wooden warship with iron armor plating.

Manifest Destiny Belief that "God's will" destined the United States to encompass all lands between the Atlantic and Pacific Oceans.

Musket Smoothbore shoulder firearm used by infantry to fire lead balls instead of pointed bullets. Usually heavy, slow to load and fire, and inaccurate beyond 100 yards (91m).

Ramparts Raised fortifications, usually walls or mounds of earth capped or covered with stone or brick.

Reconstruction The economic and political reorganization of the Confederate states following the Civil War.

Rifle Shoulder firearm with grooves cut inside the barrel to rotate and stabilize the fired bullets, allowing more accuracy. Repeating rifles held several cartridges and could be fired numerous times before reloading.

Secede To withdraw formally from an alliance or federation.

Siege To surround and attack a fortified place.

Slave A person who is the property of and wholly subject to another person.

States' rights The right of individual states to make laws on issues that do not affect national security, such as slavery or education. The Constitution gives states the right to assume powers not specifically delegated to the federal government nor forbidden to the states.

Telegraph The first form of electric transmission of messages via a wire.

Underground Railroad Secret, informal system of smuggling escaped slaves to freedom in the Northern U.S. or Canada.

Further Resources

Books

Anderson, Dale.
The Civil War in the East (1861–July 1863) (World Almanac Library of the Civil War). Milwaukee: World Almanac, 2004.

Anderson, Dale.
The Civil War in the West (1861–July 1863) (World Almanac Library of the Civil War). Milwaukee: World Almanac, 2004.

Anderson, Dale.
The Union Victory (July 1863–1865) (World Almanac Library of the Civil War). Milwaukee: World Almanac, 2004.

Bolotin, Norman, *The Civil War A to Z: A Young Readers' Guide to Over 100 People, Places and Points of Importance*, New York: Dutton Children's Books, 2002

McPherson, James M.
Fields of Fury: The American Civil War New York: Atheneum, 2002.

Rice, Earle, Jr., and Earle Rice.
Ulysses S. Grant: Defender Of The Union (Civil War Generals). Greensboro, NC: Morgan Reynolds Publishing, 2005.

Riehecky, Janet.
Ulysses S. Grant (Encyclopedia of Presidents. Second Series). CT: Children's Press, 2004.

Smith, Tamara and Stephanie Britt.
The Story Of Ulysses S. Grant. Nashville, TN: Candy Cane Press, 2005.

Stanchack, John.
Eyewitness: Civil War. Minneapolis: Compass Point, 2000.

Williams, Jean Kinney.
Ulysses S Grant. (Profiles of the Presidents). Minneapolis: Compass Point Books, 2002.

Web Sites

AmericanCivilWar.com
www.americancivilwar.com

The Civil War
www.civilwar.com

The Civil War Home Page
www.civil-war.net

CivilWarTraveler.com
www.civilwartraveler.com

The History Place: The U.S.
Civil War 1861-1865
www.historyplace.com/
civilwar

The Ulysses S. Grant
Association
www.lib.siu.edu/projects/
usgrant

Ulysses S. Grant Vital Stat
www.mscomm.com/~ulysse

The Underground Railroad
www.nationalgeographic.
com/railroad

United States Civil War
www.us-civilwar.com

The United States Civil Wa
Center
www.cwc.lsu.edu